Dear God

❧ My Prayer Journal ❧

EMILIE BARNES

HARVEST HOUSE PUBLISHERS
Eugene, Oregon 97402

Cover design by Left Coast Design, Portland, Oregon

Dear God

97 98 99 00 01 02 03 04 05 06 / QH / 10 9 8 7 6 5 4 3 2 1

Dear Parents and Grandparents,

*A*t one time in my life, I had five children under the age of five living in my home. As a young wife and mother, I soon discovered that I needed an appointment with God every day to commit my works as wife, mother, and homemaker to Him. Out of that need came *Prayers and Remembrances*, a prayer journal I put together that's a simple way to organize and make the most of your prayer time.

Since then, it's been my heart's desire to take what I've done for adults in *Prayers and Remembrances* and make it appropriate for children. Your children or grandchildren can share in the excitement of talking with God and sharing a special time with Him each day.

I think you'll find this plan easy to do and fun for the kids. Every day of the week, you'll pray for specific people and needs:

Monday	*Family*
Tuesday	*Friends*
Wednesday	*Leaders and Teachers*
Thursday	*People Who Are Sick or Having Trouble*
Friday	*Yourself*
Saturday	*Whatever Is on Your Heart*
Sunday	*Thank God for All You Have*

There are places to write specific requests and special Bible verses, as well as creative ideas for your prayer time together.

I know you'll enjoy this spiritual experience with the children or grandchildren God has graciously given you. May your blessings be great as you seek Him together.

Joyfully,

Emilie Barnes

What Is Prayer?

Prayer is talking to God. You can talk to Him anytime and anywhere because He is always listening. God hears not just the words you say, but He knows the thoughts of your heart too!

You can't see God, but He sees and hears you every day. God is your friend, and He wants you to pray. Just like you talk to your mom and dad or your grandpa and grandma or your friends, you can talk to God too.

You can talk to God about anything. Tell Him how much you love Him for all the good things He gives you to enjoy. Tell Him when you're hurt or sad. Tell Him you're sorry for the wrong things you do. He will always forgive you!

God loves you and thinks you're very special. Talk to Him today. He's waiting to hear from you!

*When I pray for you, my heart
is full of joy.*
—Philippians 1:4 TLB

Monday
Your Family

On the left-hand page, put a small photo of the person you will be praying for. On the opposite page, draw an outline of their hand. Draw a heart in the middle of the hand. As you pray for this special person, hold your hand over theirs. Even though you may be apart, your hearts beat together.

Monday

Place a photo of the person you're praying for here.

Things to Pray About

_____

_____

_____

_____

_____

_____

_____

_____

Monday

(Trace their hand here.)

Special Bible Verse

Monday

Place a photo of the person
you're praying for here.

Things to Pray About

_____

_____

_____

_____

_____

_____

_____

_____

Monday

(Trace their hand here.)

Special Bible Verse

Monday

Place a photo of the person you're praying for here.

Things to Pray About

_____

_____

_____

_____

_____

_____

_____

_____

_____

Monday

(Trace their hand here.)

Special Bible Verse

Monday

Place a photo of the person
you're praying for here.

Things to Pray About

_____

_____

_____

_____

_____

_____

_____

_____

Monday

(Trace their hand here.)

Special Bible Verse

_____

_____

_____

Monday

Place a photo of the person you're praying for here.

Things to Pray About

_____

_____

_____

_____

_____

_____

_____

_____

_____

Monday

(Trace their hand here.)

Special Bible Verse

_____

_____

_____

Monday

Place a photo of the person you're praying for here.

Things to Pray About

_____

_____

_____

_____

_____

_____

_____

_____

Monday

(Trace their hand here.)

Special Bible Verse

_____

_____

_____

Monday

Place a photo of the person you're praying for here.

Things to Pray About

_____

_____

_____

_____

_____

_____

_____

_____

Monday

(Trace their hand here.)

Special Bible Verse

Monday

Place a photo of the person you're praying for here.

Things to Pray About

_____

_____

_____

_____

_____

_____

_____

_____

Monday

(Trace their hand here.)

Special Bible Verse

Praying for Your Pets

*I*f you have a pet in your home, it's like having another member of the family! It's easy to love and care about a special animal. Maybe you have a dog who sleeps at the foot of your bed at night. Or perhaps your cat likes to snuggle with you on the couch. You might have a bird who sits on your shoulder and can say your name!

Sometimes things can happen to your pet—things that make you worry or sad. God wants you to talk to Him when that happens. The Bible says, "Give your burdens to the Lord. He will carry them" (Psalm 55:22 TLB). Here are some ways you can give your burden to Jesus by praying for your pet if he's in a scary situation.

If your pet is sick or hurt . . .

- Pray for yourself and other members of your family, that you'll do the right things in caring for your pet.

- Pray for the vet who is taking care of your pet. Ask God to help him (or her) do the very best job he can.

If your pet is lost . . .

- Pray for the people looking for your pet, that they'll search in the right places and not overlook somewhere your pet might be.

- Pray for your pet's safety. Ask God to help car drivers be extra careful if they see your pet on the road.

- Pray for the person who finds your pet, that he'll make every effort to contact you and bring your pet home.

Tuesday

Your Friends

*Whenever we pray for you we always begin
by giving thanks to God . . .*

—Colossians 1:3 TLB

Tuesday

Place a photo of your
friend here.

My Friend's Name

_____

Things to Pray About

_____
_____
_____
_____
_____

Tuesday

(Trace their hand here.)

Special Bible Verse

_____

_____

_____

Tuesday

Place a photo of your
friend here.

My Friend's Name

_____

Things to Pray About

_____
_____
_____
_____
_____

Tuesday

(Trace their hand here.)

Special Bible Verse

_____

_____

_____

Tuesday

Place a photo of your
friend here.

My Friend's Name

_____

Things to Pray About

_____

_____

_____

_____

_____

Tuesday

(Trace their hand here.)

Special Bible Verse

Tuesday

Place a photo of your
friend here.

My Friend's Name

Things to Pray About

Tuesday

(Trace their hand here.)

Special Bible Verse

_____

_____

_____

Tuesday

Place a photo of your
friend here.

My Friend's Name

_____

Things to Pray About

_____

_____

_____

_____

_____

Tuesday

(Trace their hand here.)

Special Bible Verse

_____

_____

_____

Tuesday

Place a photo of your friend here.

My Friend's Name

_____

Things to Pray About

_____
_____
_____
_____
_____

Tuesday

(Trace their hand here.)

Special Bible Verse

Tuesday

Place a photo of your friend here.

My Friend's Name

_____

Things to Pray About

_____
_____
_____
_____
_____

Tuesday

(Trace their hand here.)

Special Bible Verse

Tuesday

Place a photo of your
friend here.

My Friend's Name

_____

Things to Pray About

_____
_____
_____
_____
_____

Tuesday

(Trace their hand here.)

Special Bible Verse

_____

_____

_____

How God Answers Prayer

Wouldn't it be great if God always answered our prayers the way we wanted? We could pray for a billion dollars and *poof!* we'd be rich. But what if being rich made us stuck-up or made our friends unhappy?

God hears every prayer you pray and takes each one seriously. And often when you pray, you will get just what you ask for because it matches the very thing that God wants to do.

Sometimes, though, God doesn't answer our prayers the way we want Him to. You see, God cares a lot about our hearts. He won't say yes to prayers that are selfish (you can read more about this in James 4:1-4).

And don't be surprised if you sometimes have to wait awhile before God answers your prayers. We can't see the big picture like God can, so we sometimes don't know why there's a delay. But it happens. It happened to Mary and Martha, the sisters of Lazarus. They sent for Jesus when their brother was sick, but Jesus waited two days, until He knew Lazarus was dead, to go to them. The Bible tells us that they had to wait because Jesus wanted to do more than heal Lazarus—He wanted to raise him from the dead (John 11)!

Yes . . . no . . . wait. All three are answers to prayer, and you can always be sure God will choose the very best one.

Wednesday

Leaders and Teachers

Pray for all people. As you make your requests, plead for God's mercy upon them, and give thanks. Pray this way for kings and all others who are in authority . . .

—1 Timothy 2:1,2

Wednesday

Place a photo of the person
you're praying for here.

Name

Things to Pray About

Wednesday

(Trace their hand here.)

Special Bible Verse

_____

_____

_____

Wednesday

Place a photo of the person
you're praying for here.

Name

_____

Things to Pray About

_____
_____
_____
_____
_____

Wednesday

(Trace their hand here.)

Special Bible Verse

_____

_____

_____

Wednesday

Place a photo of the person
you're praying for here.

Name

_____

Things to Pray About

_____

_____

_____

_____

_____

Wednesday

(Trace their hand here.)

Special Bible Verse

_____

_____

_____

Place a photo of the person
you're praying for here.

Name

Things to Pray About

Wednesday

(Trace their hand here.)

Special Bible Verse

_____

_____

_____

Wednesday

Place a photo of the person you're praying for here.

Name

_____

Things to Pray About

_____

_____

_____

_____

_____

Wednesday

(Trace their hand here.)

Special Bible Verse

_____

_____

_____

Wednesday

Place a photo of the person you're praying for here.

Name

_____

Things to Pray About

_____

_____

_____

_____

_____

Wednesday

(Trace their hand here.)

Special Bible Verse

Wednesday

Place a photo of the person you're praying for here.

Name

Things to Pray About

Wednesday

(Trace their hand here.)

Special Bible Verse

_____

_____

_____

Wednesday

Place a photo of the person you're praying for here.

Name

Things to Pray About

Wednesday

(Trace their hand here.)

Special Bible Verse

_____

_____

_____

Praying for the President

*H*ow do you pray for someone you don't even know—especially someone as important as the President? Try this: If your family watches the news or reads the paper together, take special note of anything that is said about the President. Is he on a trip to another country? Does he need to make a big decision soon? Make a list and then pray about these specific things.

Here are some other ways you might pray for the President:

- Every day the President makes decisions that affect the whole country. Pray that God would guide him to make the best choices for all of the people.

- People who have a lot of power are sometimes tempted to do wrong things. Pray that the President would recognize evil and stay away from it.

- The President is often involved in long meetings with people who have different ideas than he does. Pray that he would be able to get along with all kinds of people.

- It is easy to think you're better than other people when you are the most powerful person in the world. Pray that the President would be a fair and humble man.

- The President is very busy. Pray for his family and the time he spends with them.

Thursday

People Who Are Sick or Having Trouble

Are any among you suffering? They should keep on praying about it.

—James 5:13

Thursday

Place a photo of the person
you're praying for here.

Dear God, please help
this person:

_____

_____

_____

_____

_____

_____

_____

Thursday

(Trace their hand here.)

Special Bible Verse

_____

_____

_____

Thursday

Place a photo of the person
you're praying for here.

Dear God, please help
this person:

_____

_____

_____

_____

_____

_____

_____

Thursday

(Trace their hand here.)

Special Bible Verse

_____

_____

_____

Thursday

Place a photo of the person you're praying for here.

Dear God, please help this person:

_____

_____

_____

_____

_____

_____

_____

Thursday

(Trace their hand here.)

Special Bible Verse

_____

_____

_____

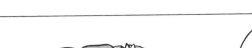

Thursday

Place a photo of the person you're praying for here.

Dear God, please help this person:

_____

_____

_____

_____

_____

_____

_____

Thursday

(Trace their hand here.)

Special Bible Verse

Thursday

Place a photo of the person
you're praying for here.

Dear God, please help
this person:

_____

_____

_____

_____

_____

_____

_____

Thursday

(Trace their hand here.)

Special Bible Verse

Thursday

Place a photo of the person you're praying for here.

Dear God, please help this person:

_____

_____

_____

_____

_____

_____

_____

_____

Thursday

(Trace their hand here.)

Special Bible Verse

Thursday

Place a photo of the person you're praying for here.

Dear God, please help this person:

_____

_____

_____

_____

_____

_____

_____

Thursday

(Trace their hand here.)

Special Bible Verse

Thursday

Place a photo of the person you're praying for here.

Dear God, please help this person:

_____

_____

_____

_____

_____

_____

_____

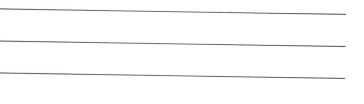

Thursday

(Trace their hand here.)

Special Bible Verse

_____

_____

_____

Nice Things to Do
for a Sick Friend

Being sick is B-O-R-I-N-G. But one good thing about being sick is that people do special things for you. Here are a few nice things you can do for a friend who isn't feeling well.

🌱 Find a basket (an old Easter basket is perfect) and turn it into a special "get well" basket. Line the basket with the comic strip section of the newspaper. Then fill it with crossword puzzles, games, or mazes you make yourself. Roll your puzzles up and tie each with a pretty ribbon. Do you have a jigsaw puzzle you're finished with? Add it to the basket. If your friend isn't contagious, loan her your favorite stuffed animal or toy. Or make a family of finger puppets out of scraps of fabric from your mom's sewing basket (ask first!). Use your imagination. Anything that makes you happy when you're sick will make your friend happy too.

🌱 If you have flowers in your garden, pick a beautiful bouquet. If not, draw some flowers on a piece of thick paper. Fold the paper in half and write a note telling your friend you are praying for her.

🌱 Write a fill-in-the-blank story for your friend to finish.

🌱 Make up songs or sing songs you already know into a tape recorder and give the tape to your friend.

🌱 Go to the library and check out a few books you know your friend would enjoy: horse stories, mysteries, etc. You could read a chapter or two together. *The Chronicles of Narnia* by C.S. Lewis are great stories to read aloud.

Friday

Yourself

I know you will answer me, O God!
Yes, listen as I pray.

—Psalm 17:6 TLB

Friday

My
Picture

Friday

Today I'm going to
pray for me . . .

_____

_____

_____

_____

_____

_____

_____

_____

_____

_____

Special Bible Verse

_____

_____

_____

Friday

Today I'm going to
pray for me . . .

_____

_____

_____

_____

_____

_____

_____

_____

_____

_____

Special Bible Verse

_____

_____

_____

_____

Friday

Today I'm going to pray for me . . .

_____

_____

_____

_____

_____

_____

_____

_____

Special Bible Verse

_____

_____

_____

Friday

Today I'm going to
pray for me . . .

_____

_____

_____

_____

_____

_____

_____

_____

Special Bible Verse

_____

_____

_____

Friday

Today I'm going to
pray for me . . .

_____

_____

_____

_____

_____

_____

_____

_____

Special Bible Verse

_____

_____

_____

Friday

Today I'm going to
pray for me . . .

_____

_____

_____

_____

_____

_____

_____

_____

_____

Special Bible Verse

_____

_____

_____

Friday

Today I'm going to pray for me . . .

_____

_____

_____

_____

_____

_____

_____

Special Bible Verse

_____

_____

_____

Friday

Today I'm going to
pray for me . . .

_____

_____

_____

_____

_____

_____

_____

_____

Special Bible Verse

_____

_____

_____

Friday

Today I'm going to
pray for me . . .

_____

_____

_____

_____

_____

_____

_____

_____

_____

Special Bible Verse

_____

_____

_____

Friday

Today I'm going to pray for me . . .

_____

_____

_____

_____

_____

_____

_____

_____

Special Bible Verse

_____

_____

_____

Friday

Today I'm going to pray for me . . .

_____

_____

_____

_____

_____

_____

_____

_____

Special Bible Verse

_____

_____

_____

Friday

Today I'm going to
pray for me . . .

_____
_____
_____
_____
_____
_____
_____
_____
_____
_____

Special Bible Verse

_____
_____
_____

Friday

Today I'm going to
pray for me . . .

_____

_____

_____

_____

_____

_____

_____

Special Bible Verse

_____

_____

_____

Friday

Today I'm going to pray for me . . .

_____

_____

_____

_____

_____

_____

_____

_____

Special Bible Verse

_____

_____

_____

Friday

Today I'm going to
pray for me . . .

_____

_____

_____

_____

_____

_____

_____

_____

Special Bible Verse

_____

_____

_____

When Should I Pray?

It's good to have a special time to talk to God every day. But remember that God wants us to talk to Him all through the day too. He wants to share every part of our lives. Here are some other times when you can talk with Him. You might look these verses up in your own Bible.

❦ *When you're in trouble and when you're happy*
Are any among you suffering? They should keep on praying about it. And those who have reason to be thankful should continually sing praises to the Lord (James 5:13).

❦ *When people are unkind to you*
Pray for those who hurt you (Luke 6:28).

❦ *When you're sick*
Are any among you sick? They should call for the elders of the church and have them pray over them, anointing them with oil in the name of the Lord (James 5:14).

❦ *When you've done something wrong*
Confess your sins to each other and pray for each other so that you may be healed (James 5:16).

❦ *Anytime you think of a Christian friend*
Be persistent in your prayers for all Christians everywhere (Ephesians 6:18).

❦ *All of the time!*
Keep on praying (1 Thessalonians 5:17).

Saturday

Pray for Whatever Is on Your Heart

*Give your burdens to the Lord, and he
will take care of you.*

—Psalm 55:22

Saturday

Jesus, these things are
on my heart:

_____
_____
_____
_____
_____
_____
_____
_____
_____

Special Bible Verse

_____
_____
_____

Saturday

Thank You, Jesus,
for Your answers:

_____
_____
_____
_____
_____
_____
_____
_____
_____
_____
_____
_____
_____
_____
_____
_____
_____

Saturday

Jesus, these things are on my heart:

_____

_____

_____

_____

_____

_____

_____

_____

_____

_____

Special Bible Verse

_____

_____

_____

Saturday

Thank You, Jesus, for Your answers:

_____

_____

_____

_____

_____

_____

_____

_____

_____

_____

_____

_____

_____

_____

_____

_____

_____

Saturday

Jesus, these things are
on my heart:

_____

_____

_____

_____

_____

_____

_____

_____

Special Bible Verse

_____

_____

_____

Saturday

Thank You, Jesus,
for Your answers:

_____

_____

_____

_____

_____

_____

_____

_____

_____

_____

_____

_____

_____

_____

_____

_____

Saturday

Jesus, these things are
on my heart:

_____

_____

_____

_____

_____

_____

_____

_____

_____

Special Bible Verse

_____

_____

_____

Saturday

Thank You, Jesus,
for Your answers:

_____

_____

_____

_____

_____

_____

_____

_____

_____

_____

_____

_____

_____

_____

_____

_____

_____

Saturday

Jesus, these things are
on my heart:

_____

_____

_____

_____

_____

_____

_____

_____

Special Bible Verse

_____

_____

_____

Saturday

Thank You, Jesus, for Your answers:

_____
_____
_____
_____
_____
_____
_____
_____
_____
_____
_____
_____
_____
_____
_____
_____
_____
_____

Saturday

Jesus, these things are
on my heart:

_____

_____

_____

_____

_____

_____

_____

_____

Special Bible Verse

_____

_____

_____

Saturday

Thank You, Jesus, for Your answers:

_____

_____

_____

_____

_____

_____

_____

_____

_____

_____

_____

_____

_____

_____

_____

Saturday

Jesus, these things are on my heart:

_____

_____

_____

_____

_____

_____

_____

_____

Special Bible Verse

_____

_____

_____

Saturday

Thank You, Jesus,
for Your answers:

_____

_____

_____

_____

_____

_____

_____

_____

_____

_____

_____

_____

_____

_____

_____

_____

_____

Saturday

Jesus, these things are
on my heart:

_____

_____

_____

_____

_____

_____

_____

_____

Special Bible Verse

_____

_____

_____

Saturday

Thank You, Jesus,
for Your answers:

_____
_____
_____
_____
_____
_____
_____
_____
_____
_____
_____
_____
_____
_____
_____

In Jesus' Name

Have you ever wondered why we end our prayers "In Jesus' name, Amen"?

Jesus tells us we are to pray using His name: "Ask, using my name, and you will receive, and your cup of joy will overflow" (John 16:24 TLB; see also John 14:13,14 and John 15:16). When we pray "in Jesus' name," what we are saying is, "Jesus, I want whatever it is You want. I know You have a plan, and I want You to do what You know is right." Those three words remind us that we want our prayers to be in line with God's plans for us.

And what about "amen"? That's a word that comes from the Hebrew language, and it basically means "so let it be." We use it at the end of our prayers to say we agree with what's been said and we believe it with our whole heart. That's why sometimes when you're praying in a group, others will say "amen" after someone has finished praying. They are letting everyone know that they are praying for the same thing.

Sunday

Thank God for All You Have

Give thanks to the Lord and proclaim
his greatness. Let the whole world
know what he has done.

—1 Chronicles 16:8

Sunday

Five Things I'm Thankful For . . .

1. _____

   _____

2. _____

   _____

3. _____

   _____

4. _____

   _____

5. _____

   _____

Special Bible Verse

_____

_____

_____

Sunday

Five Things I'm Thankful For . . .

1. _____
   _____

2. _____
   _____

3. _____
   _____

4. _____
   _____

5. _____
   _____

Special Bible Verse

_____

_____

_____

Sunday

Five Things I'm Thankful For . . .

1. _____
   _____
2. _____
   _____
3. _____
   _____
4. _____
   _____
5. _____
   _____

Special Bible Verse

_____
_____
_____

Sunday

Five Things I'm Thankful For . . .

1. _____
_____

2. _____
_____

3. _____
_____

4. _____
_____

5. _____
_____

Special Bible Verse

_____

_____

_____

Sunday

Five Things I'm Thankful For . . .

1. _____
   _____
2. _____
   _____
3. _____
   _____
4. _____
   _____
5. _____
   _____

Special Bible Verse

_____
_____
_____

Sunday

Five Things I'm Thankful For . . .

1. _____

_____

2. _____

_____

3. _____

_____

4. _____

_____

5. _____

_____

Special Bible Verse

_____

_____

_____

Sunday

Five Things I'm Thankful For . . .

1. _____
   _____

2. _____
   _____

3. _____
   _____

4. _____
   _____

5. _____
   _____

Special Bible Verse

_____

_____

_____

Sunday

Five Things I'm Thankful For . . .

1. _____
_____

2. _____
_____

3. _____
_____

4. _____
_____

5. _____
_____

Special Bible Verse

_____
_____
_____

Sunday

Five Things I'm
Thankful For . . .

1. _____

_____

2. _____

_____

3. _____

_____

4. _____

_____

5. _____

_____

Special Bible Verse

_____

_____

_____

Sunday

Five Things I'm Thankful For . . .

1. _____
   _____
2. _____
   _____
3. _____
   _____
4. _____
   _____
5. _____
   _____

Special Bible Verse

_____
_____
_____

Sunday

Five Things I'm
Thankful For . . .

1. _____
_____

2. _____
_____

3. _____
_____

4. _____
_____

5. _____
_____

Special Bible Verse

_____
_____
_____

Sunday

Five Things I'm Thankful For . . .

1. _____
   _____

2. _____
   _____

3. _____
   _____

4. _____
   _____

5. _____
   _____

Special Bible Verse

_____

_____

_____

This is my little prayer book,
And here is what I'll do—
I'll write my thoughts and
prayer requests
Before each day is through.

❧ ❧ ❧

The pages will fall open
To the special day of prayer
For friends and family and others
Who need God's tender care.

❧ ❧ ❧

Thank You, heavenly Father,
For listening when I pray,
Your warm love always guides me
In all I do and say.